T0196588

DO YOUR OWN TRIBUNAL HEARING OR FORMAL MEETING

Sadick H Keshavjee LLB. Hon. (Lon)

Published Author, Trainer
Retired
Certified Arbitrator
Chartered Governance Professional
Chartered Secretary
Commissioner for oaths
Paralegal

Order this book online at www.trafford.com
or email orders@trafford.com

Most Trafford titles are also available at major online book retailers.

Print information available on the last page.

ISBN: 978-1-6987-0451-7 (sc)

Trafford rev.   12/02/2021

North America & international
toll-free: 844-688-6899 (USA & Canada)
fax: 812 355 4082

PREFACE

Whilst this is not a substitute for Legal, Financial or Tax advice this booklet highlights material, in lay persons terms (as much as feasible), issues which are highlighted in my previous books (also available in digital format) but that needs to have special mention for the lay person to have a deeper understanding.

See www.cometetrain.com

These topics are also part of the authors education, experience and training programs he has conducted for various professional bodies.

Lawyers, accountants, financial planners are are indispensable in a well run democracy but are the subject of jokes

It is in this vein that I've added 'lawyer jokes' sourced from "Lawyers, Jokes, and Anecdotes" by Andrews Mc Meel Publishing edited by Patrick Regan 2001.

This has been interspersed with 'words of wisdom' so as to allow for distractions from a subject that can be dry, albeit very useful.

The intended audience is a person living in a common law country that was under the influence of the British legal system. 'when the sun never set on the British Empire'

I wish to thank the the former AG of Kenya Hon Amos Wako and Prof Amyn Sajoo of the Simon Frazer University for their forewords to my earlier editions of my books for which this material has been sourced.

Sadick H Keshavjee LLB (Hon)

Certified Arbitrator Certified member Chartered Governance Insitute/Chartered Secretary

Author and Online trainer, Commissioner for oaths

CONTENTS

CHAPTER 1

EQUITABLE REMEDIES (PROCEDURAL FAIRNESS)

Such remedies are based on equitable principles and a brief background as to the historical origins are appropriate here.

There were two main developments in the common law in of England in the in early centuries. One was the Provision of Oxford (1258) which had the effect of several provisions restricting the writ (A document in the crowns name commanding the person to whom it is addressed to do or forbear from doing some act. This could be issued by the "royal" courts in existence at that time. The second development was the statute of the Westminster which provided that the new writs could only be issued which were similar to those in existence before the Provisions of Oxford.

The fact that Common Law required the right form of action and that one could only obtain damages and the fact that most people "in high places" could defy the law was of concern to the King. More so as he was considered the "Fountain of Justice". The King delegated these matters to the Chancellor who was thought to be the "Keeper of the Kings Conscience". He in turn set up a Chancery Courts which operated in different way from the common law Courts. If the Chancellor was satisfied after persistent questioning by him that the defendant had done wrong and that his conscience was burdened by guilt, he would order the defendant to make good his wrong and so clear his conscience.

This type of justice which had no binding rules became known as' Equity'. Each Chancellor was able to give judgment based on his own conscience and thus resulted in the expression that "Equity varies with the length of the Chancellors foot".

The separate systems were fused, the Chancery Courts being abolished.

Over a period of time, however, Equity built up its own series of rules and precedents.

The Maxims ("concise truths") of Equity cover the general principles or guidelines which evolved in the Court of Chancery.

Well known example of maxims of Equity:

HE WHO COMES TO EQUITY MUST COME WITH CLEAN HANDS.

A plaintiff who seeks equitable relief must have acted fairly towards the defendant.

A tenant cannot get specific performance of a contract for a lease if he has already breached his obligations.

EQUITY IMPUTES AN INTENTION TO FULFIL AN OBLIGATION

Where a person is obliged to do some act, and does some other act which could be regarded as a performance of it, then it will be so regarded in Equity.

EQUITY IS EQUALITY

Where two or more persons are entitled to an interest in the same property in a will then the principles of Equity is equal division, if there is no good reason for any other basis for division.

EQUITY LOOKS AT THE INTENT RATHER THAN THE FORM

The minute you read something you can't understand, you can be almost sure it was drawn up by a lawyer.

CHAPTER 2
CODE OF ETHICS FOR A TRIBUNAL

Herewith is a summary for rules that if breached can be a grounds for objection or appeal.

1. *The tribunal shall be fair.*
2. *Act with integrity.*
3. *Act impartially and independently.*
4. *Treat participants with courtesy, fairness and integrity.*
5. *Full disclosure to prevent an apprehension of bias.*
6. *Must be able and competent*
7. *Shall complete hearing after the appointment.*
8. *Communicate equally with the parties.*
9. *Keep all matters confidential.*

A lawyer is someone who approaches every subject with an open mouth.

CHAPTER 3

PUTTING PEN TO PAPER

Here are some rules for a party to follow in the event written submissions are required.

This process is not rocket science. But it does require clear thinking and common sense coupled with brevity.

It should be like a mini skirt- long enough to cover the subject matter but short enough to be interesting.

SUBMISSIONS

The Applicant is the person making the claim,

HINTS

15 PAGES GOOD

HEADINGS

KEEP COPIES

ATTACH PHOTOS

CHANGE FONTS

Attach affidavits of witnesses

Use letter of refusal as a starting point

Attach psychologists report

Raise objections in a timely manner

Use FedEx (good tracking)

Don't hide facts

Keep notes of meetings

Ask for more time

Everything claimed must be documented and evidenced

Use alternative arguments eg time to cure etc

May need to apply for "stay" court proceedings whilst the arbitration proceeds

There's a new word processing software program for lawyers you can change the font, but when you print it out the words always show up in fine print

CHAPTER 4
STEPS IN THE APPEAL ADVOCACY PROCESS

Three key words are important, preparation, preparation and preparation!

i. *One should determine what law and policies apply with regard to the particular hearing. (I.e. the enabling legislation, rules of procedure, as it is important to ensure that the tribunal has the jurisdiction authority and powers to conduct the hearing)*

ii. *Determine from the rules, stages in the process and deadlines*

iii. *Determine who makes the decision at each stage*

iv. *Determine the concerns of other stakeholders (parties not directly connected to the hearing, but that could be affected by this hearing.)*

v. *- Tailor submissions*

- Identify issues questions of fact, what laws apply and the correct policy to apply. (preliminary procedures, disclosure and legal research).

- Determine burden and standard of proof See chapter on evidence)

Collect evidence and identify witnesses with subpoenas if need be

- Research the law

- Organise materials. Binder indexed with book of authorities

- Court precedents to support arguments.

- Never mislead the tribunal and do not take extreme positions unless provable. Focus on the most convincing issues and arguments.

- Show respect.

- Address the tribunal.

vi. *Obtain reasons for the decisions.*

A useful acronym is KISS (Keep It Short and Simple)!

Wife: you just don't care anymore
Husband: you're upset. Let's buy something to make you feel better
Wife: like what?
Husband: how about a trip to the Orient?
Wife: no
Husband: A BMW?

Wife: no
Husband: well what do you want?
Wife: A divorce
Husband: I wasn't planning on spending that much.!!!

WORDS OF WISDOM

"One of the most striking differences between a cat and a lie is that a cat has only 9 lives -Mark Twain"

"I know I am strengthened as I seek to make truth my personal reality"- Wayne Dyer

QUESTION: What is your name?
ANSWER: Mary Ann O'Donnell
QUESTION: And what is your marital status?
ANSWER: Fair

CHAPTER 5
EVIDENCE FOR THE NOVICE

EVIDENCE IN HEARING *(Credit to Chartered Institute of Arbitrators of UK)*

A tribunal hearing is not a court hearing. But an overview of the basic rules can be helpful so that you are not cought unawares, with a sneaky opponent.

- *The tribunal should not, unless all parties agree, make him or her inquisitor (or "enter into the arena" as Lord Denning would call it. That is, only clarification questions should be asked and not conduct the hearing), the tribunal should also not take evidence behind a party's back. The rules of evidence which are applied in the civil courts also bind a tribunal*
- *Evidence presented must be admissible*
- *The most important category of inadmissible evidence is irrelevant material. Only evidence that is relevant to issues in the hearing. Relevance depends upon the particular facts of each case.*
- *The parties must take care to keep the hearing firmly focussed upon issues which have a direct bearing on the claim, and ought not to permit a marginal exploration into matters not connected.(i.e. go on a fishing expedition)*
- *The other main categories of inadmissible evidence are as follows:*
  - *Opinion evidence: the opinion of a witness is inadmissible unless he is an expert (by qualification or experience in that subject)*
  - *Hearsay evidence: in general, only facts within the direct knowledge of a witness are relevant, not those he has been told by others.*
  - *Privileged communications: confidential documents passing between parties and their legal advisers.*

The courts are reluctant to overturn rulings on the grounds of the mere wrongful reception or rejection of evidence. Provided the tribunal acts honestly and in a judicial manner (for instance, by affording all parties the opportunity to make submissions before a ruling is made), he is not by reason of that ruling alone guilty of misconduct, even though the ruling may be contrary to law, at least if the error does not go to the root of the question he/she has to decide on:

<u>*Conditional admissibility*</u>

- *Questions of admissibility are normally dealt with by an immediate ruling by the tribunal*
    - o *In those circumstances he may admit the evidence "de bene esse", that is to say :on a provisional basis", so that depending on what later evidence reveals, he may eventually decide to admit the contentious evidence, or to exclude and ignore it in reaching his ruling.*

<u>*Weight of the evidence*</u>

- *Evidence that is admitted in hearing must still be weighed by the tribunal in order to determine how much force should be given to it. All the circumstances of the evidence and the manner in which it is given are material; but finally the tribunal must bring his own common sense, experience and judgement to bear in order to decide, for instance, which of two conflicting witnesses is telling the truth, or what are the proper inferences to be drawn from the things he has seen and heard.*
- *Direct evidence of a fact is usually more weighty than hearsay evidence of the same fact, and is often more convincing than mere circumstantial evidence*
- *Circumstantial evidence can point just as clearly as direct evidence in favour of a particular conclusion.*
- *Expert witnesses led by one party may seem better qualified or more authoritative than those produced by the other.*
- *Witnesses who have a direct interest in the outcome of the hearing may have to be treated with more suspicion than wholly independent witnesses.*
- *It is usually for the party making the claim in the hearing to prove by evidence to the tribunal's satisfaction each component part of the claim. The burden of proof is said to lie on the party asserting its entitlement to relief.*
- *If the evidence does not persuade the tribunal on all the disputed issues then the claim will likely fail.*
- *If the evidence on an issue or in the claim is of equal value so that the tribunal simply cannot decide between the contentions of either side, then the party on whom the burden of proof lies will likely fail.*
- *Within a single hearing there may well be issues in respect of which the burden of proof falls on different parties, for instance, the claimant may allege negligence and the respondent "contributory" (to what extent the claimant contributed to the event)negligence; the claimant may allege a contract and the respondent may allege its invalidity on the grounds of fraud, misrepresentation or mistake.*

- *Sometimes, a rule of common law, statute or an agreement between the parties will throw the burden of proving an issue on to the respondent:*
- *In theory, the burden of proof can be further broken down into the evidential burden, i.e. the duty to produce sufficient evidence from which the tribunal may safely conclude that the thing contended for is true; and the persuasive burden, i.e. the duty to prove to the tribunal's satisfaction that the thing contended for is in fact true.*
- *The practical importance of this distinction is that if the evidential burden is not discharged then that aspect of the hearing should proceed no further, since there is insufficient evidence on which to base a finding of fact; and if it does proceed, the losing party may attempt to impeach the ruling on the grounds that the evidence was inadequate to support a finding on that point.*

Standard of proof

- *The standard of proof is the degree of certainty which the tribunal must hold before finding that the burden of proof has been discharged.*
- *In hearings this is normally defined as the balance of probabilities. In other words, the party bearing the burden of proof must prove that the thing contended for is more likely than not to be true.*
- *Although expressed in objective terms, the standard of proof is applied in a flexible and subjective way in that the degree of certainty required for the tribunal to be satisfied "on balance" will vary according to the gravity of the allegation made; the consequences of accepting it to be true; the probability or otherwise of the allegation; the size of the claim; and so forth.*
- *Even if unlawful or criminal conduct is alleged, the tribunal must not apply the criminal standard of proof "beyond reasonable doubt"; but must apply the "balance of probability" test, recognizing that it will be more difficult for a party to pass that test where serious allegations are made:*
- *Where no evidence is necessary things that are not in issue, either because they form the "common ground" between the parties (as will be apparent from the pleadings or statement of case) or because they are formally admitted need not to be proved by evidence.*
- *Things of which "judicial notice" is taken also need not be proved by evidence. Such things are deemed to be within the inherent knowledge of the tribunal.*
- *"Notorious facts" may, for example, be judicially noticed, as being so well established that no sensible person could dispute them:*
- *Tribunals may use their general knowledge of the relevant trade without putting the matters on which they rely to the parties*

- *If, however, the tribunal has particular knowledge of the events which are the subject matter of the dispute, he is bound to tell the parties of that knowledge, so as to give them an opportunity to call evidence to support or contradict his understanding of the facts.*
- *Presumptions are substitutes or partial substitutes for evidence which entitle the tribunal to pronounce without complete or any evidence on a particular issue. As such, they are aids to determination.*
- *The tribunal may be obliged to find that a certain fact exists unless it is proved by evidence to the contrary that it does not exist:*
- *He may be obliged to find that a certain fact exists unless prima facie evidence in rebuttal is adduced to cast doubt on its existence:*
- *The tribunal may be entitled (but not bound) to find that a fact exists. There is sufficient circumstantial evidence from which the fact in question may (but not must) be inferred:*
  - *Legal professional privilege*
  - *Communications between client and legal advisor*

Such communications, whether oral or in writing, will be privileged from disclosure provided the following conditions were fulfilled at the time they were made:

a. *The communication is made to or by the legal advisor in his professional capacity;*
b. *The person retained to advise falls within the classes of "legal adviser" recognized by the privilege:*
c. *The communication is made in connection with the giving or receiving of advise within the ordinary scope of the legal adviser's employ:*
d. *The relationship of client and legal adviser exists between the parties, or is in reasonable contemplation:*
e. *The parties intend that the communication remain confidential as between themselves:*

Communications with third parties:

a. *the communication was intended to be confidential as between the maker and the recipient;*
b. *Some litigation, whether civil or criminal, and whether in the ordinary courts or by hearing, was in existence or was "reasonably contemplated" or "in definite prospect";*
c. *The dominant purpose for the obtaining or coming into existence of the communication was to assist in fighting that litigation:*

This discretion subsists even where the party seeking to use the evidence has been guilty of no wrongdoing in obtaining it:

"Wrongful" inspection or copying of an opponent's privileged documents is however likely lead to the court issuing an injunction against the wrongdoer from using what he has obtained by that method:

Waiver of legal professional privilege

a. *Legal professional privilege is a PRIVATE privilege. Thus it is personal and not proprietary. The client is therefore entitled to reveal to the tribunal the contents of a communication in which he holds the privilege, and may sometimes be deemed to have made that waiver impliedly, by referring to privileged documents or conversations in interlocutory proceedings, points of claim or other correspondence.*

In practice parties to litigation are compelled to disclose privileged material.

Public interest privilege

An tribunal must not under any circumstances order a person to disclose information which it <u>would be contrary to the public interest to force him to reveal</u>. Similarly he must not allow a party to put in evidence information which is covered by such "<u>public interest immunity</u>"

Claimants to immunity

The usual claimant to public immunity privilege will be a government department or other limb or the Crown. In very limited circumstances, however, a non-governmental agency may be able to establish the immunity.

Proof of relevancy

The party seeing to obtain or to use the information for which the immunity is claimed must first show that the information is likely to be relevant to some question in the hearing:

Proof of a public interest

No immunity attaches on the mere ground that the information sought was given or received in confidence. Some public interest in preserving its secrecy must be found: the tribunal ought not to accept a claim to immunity based upon purely private grounds:

Once relevancy and a recognized public interest are shown, the tribunal proceeds to balance the public interests described. This involves a great deal of discretion

The tribunal is not allowed to inspect the thing for which the privilege is claimed unless and until it concludes, having heard argument upon the balance of interests, that the scales are evenly balanced.

Journalistic sources:

Journalists and their associated staff have a special, statutory, immunity from compulsion to reveal the source of information which has been supplied to them in confidence and which they have used in a publication or broadcast:

> *In the course of hearing proceedings, no person can usually be compelled to produce any document or to answer any questions if such document or answer any question if such document or answer would have a tendency to expose him to a real risk of prosecution for an offence under the law. This is the common law privilege against self-incrimination. And is connected with the general right of silence which suspects possess in criminal cases. It is the English equivalent of the United States' Fifth Amendment.*

The tribunal is probably under no duty to remind the witness that he may be entitled to the privilege, though it is sensible to have a reminder when it is fairly clear that the witness may incriminate himself or his spouse by giving the evidence requested of him.

It is wise to entitle "without prejudice" a letter or conversation which is a genuine attempt to settle a dispute, but the absence of that title will not necessarily be fatal to the communication's being protected by the privilege:

The privilege will however be denied to a letter which contains a "without prejudice" title if, on closer examination by the court, it proves to be not part of a genuine attempt to settle an existing dispute:

Whether or not without prejudice communications lead to a settlement of the dispute, the contents of those communications cannot be ordered disclosed to persons who were not involved in their making or receipt, and cannot be used in evidence by such persons, without the consent of all the parties to them:

If without prejudice communications lead to a settlement of the dispute, they become admissible in evidence between the parties to them for the purpose of establishing the existence and terms of the settlement, and for enforcing it through the courts. If however the communications prove fruitless and the dispute proceeds to trial, they are admissible, if at all, only on the question of costs at the conclusion of the judgment.

A lawyer died in poverty and the townspeople approached the judge to ask for dollar to bury the man. "a dollar remarked the judge." "here's $20 Go bury twenty of them."

CHAPTER 6
HEARING OF THE CASE –

This chapter will give some useful pointers as to how to take part in this process. You do not have to be a "Perry Mason" to successfully play this game. Here as some 'dos' and don'ts'

Opening addresses

They are made in such hearings and there is value in setting the scene to put the legal and factual issues in context. There is no standard format.

Things to avoid:

a. *Overstatement*
   This is not the time to try to 'sell your case". Rather, assist and inform the tribunal about your case. Moderation is the key.

b. *Avoid too much detail*
   This is not the time to present your evidence. It is a map of your case where you introduce your story and cast of witnesses so the tribunal should know who you are calling, when and why.

   The tribunal has your trial agenda and knows what to expect and what to expect as the evidence unfolds.

c. *Argument*
   This is not the place for argument, which should be left for closing. You are only setting the case for the tribunal.

   This is also not the time to anticipate defences therefore DO:

   - *Provide a broad context*
   - *What is the trial about?*
   - *What is your theory of the case?*
   - *Without using legalese tell them why your client is in court.*
   - *Give a factual and legal context in which to consider the evidence.*
   - *Introduce the parties*
   - *State the cause of action*

- State the facts
- Direct the tribunal to particular points (eg "She was the only person not drinking at the party")
- Use exhibits in your opening, even a clause in a contract
- Have a prepared legal brief on the law or an outline of the legal issues with copies of the leading cases
- You can refer to defences raised and defuse key weaknesses in your case and on which the defendant will rely
- Outline the relief sought. Tie the quantum of damages to the facts and evidence that will be presented

End with:

"That concludes the opening and with the leave of this tribunal I would now like to call my first witness"

DEFENDANTS OPENING:

- Should be short and to the point
- No need to review the cause of action, the facts of the case or the law
- Rather, concentrate on a few legal or factual issues, and clarify the defendant's position thereon.
- Then, highlight and outline the details of witnesses as in the case of the plaintiff

Therefore outline of the "who, what and when" of the case and save the attacks for closing

- Story telling is a powerful tool.
- Be succinct and helpful

A petite lawyer, appearing as a witness in a messy divorce proceeding was confronted by an ox of an opposing lawyer, who asked what she did for a living.

"I am an attorney", she said

"Hey, little lady—I could pick you up and put you in my back pocket!" he laughed.

"Probably," was the reply, "but then you'd have more legal knowledge in your pants than you ever had in your head."

CHAPTER 7

CLOSING ARGUMENTS

- 80%-90 % of the closing arguments should have been prepared before the trial starts (cases to rely on, organisation of the argument, and evidence in support of arguments).
- The last 10% can be on evidence adduced which can never be predicted accurately.
- A book of case authorities is prepared, properly bound and tabbed with highlighting.
- Copies for each tribunal member and for opposing counsel.

Things to AVOID IN CLOSINGS:

- Do not misstate the evidence
- Inform the tribunal of all pertinent authority
- Do not refer to facts not in evidence
- Do not use impassioned rhetoric ("reason" rather)
- Do not state your beliefs, let the facts and the law speak for them
- Avoid personal attacks

THEREFORE;

- A good closing meshes the facts, the law and policy.
- Be flexible so as to fit the argument to the case as long as there is a structure

For example:

Opening paragraph
- Statements of the points in issue

Issue 1: Review applicable community/society evidence and law relating thereto
Conclusion (strongest first)

"That concludes my submission on the first issue"

- Convince tribunal that your interpretation is more compelling
- Highlight particular, important evidence
- Resolve disputes presented by evidence

- Cite corroboration and consistency (evidence which confirms or supports a theory or finding)
- Cite inconsistencies, bias contradictions and look for confirmations of your case
- Expand on undisputed facts. Concentrate on credibility
- Use visual aids where possible
- Present a crisp convincing case.
- Blend all pieces together

- Present your argument before attacking the other side's position and exhibits
- Explain the law and apply it to the facts to distinguish a case on the facts or challenge it on the law
- Keep it short.
- Integrate the quoted proposition with facts of this case and show direct application
- This is not a story- state position at beginning of argument without narrating the whole case
- Use direct quotes

RIGHT OF REPLY:

- Last word is important
- Capture theme in a short strong statement
- Do not respond to a whole list of minor errors
- Deal with major misstatements of the law or facts

A verbal contract isn't worth the paper it's written on.

CHAPTER 8

EXAMINATION AND CROSS EXAMINATION (X)

After preliminary issues have been deal with and after opening statements the parties actually present their evidence the usual order being:

i. The evidence of the party who initiated the proceedings
ii. Evidence of any other parties with a similar interest in the outcome
iii. Evidence of the opposing parties
iv. Includes questioning of witnesses by the parties or their reps

The examination-in-chief

The witness may be questioned by other parties whose interest or position is similar. In the exam in chief parties are expected to ask 'open questions' ie invite the witness to provide an independent response. It does not suggest the answer that the questioner is looking for nor does it contain crucial facts or conclusions that the questioner wants the witness to confirm. It does not put words in the witness's mouth.

Leading questions are allowed only in non-controversial matters like undisputed background facts or points where the witness needs clarification. Then the X takes place

The importance of the cross examination (X) is overrated. Preparation involves gathering info about the opposing witness and their evidence. So the prep aims at structuring the X so as to get info from the witness that you need disclosed and not info that you don't want to have raised. Control of the process is crucial: you determine the agenda and you ask the questions.

PURPOSE of the Cross Examination (X):

1. To discredit the testimony of the said witness
2. To discredit the unfavorable testimony of other witnesses
3. To corroborate favorable testimony of other witnesses
4. To contribute independently to the favourable dev of your own case.

1. *To bring forth favorable testimony from the witness AND discredit unfavorable testimony from the said witness*

   The aim is not to" destroy "the witness

   They can get angry but you should be polite, sincere and with integrity. Therefore, follow the help me out approach

   Know your goals

   Why has the witness been called?

   How will he help their case?

   How can he hurt your case?

   Based on this info you can select areas for the X

   Know the evidence. E.g. from the discovery process and documents, witness statements. There is no obligation to speak.

   (With leave) you may examine for discovery the witness. You can order the production of relevant documents.

   Have a witness be present during discovery.

   At the hearing, listen carefully to each witness. New avenues may reveal themselves.

   Visit the scene.

2. *Know yourself.*
   Don't appear fake.

3. *Why the X*
   It is not a "must". If he has not hurt your case do not X
   But it is necessary to challenge contradictory evidence.
   So present this contradictory evidence (Rule in Browning v. Dunn)

PRINCIPLES

1. *Be brief*
2. *Keep it short (one line per question)*
   It is difficult to evade a simple, direct question
3. *Don't use leading questions (a question that prompts or encourages the desired answer)*
4. *Know when to stop (once they have been discredited, stop)*
5. *Do not quarrel with the witness*
6. *Plan your questions. Be subtle and indirect*
7. *Listen carefully to the witness*
   Has the question been answered? If not, ask again.

Silent spells during submissions allow issues to be digested by the audience

8. *Start safe and finish strong*
   Start in a safe area (where you know what the answers s/b. Avoid negative last impressions.
9. *Ask not only the right question but ask it the right way.*
10. *Putting it all together.*
11. *You tell the witness the facts you want. Cross refer the facts to them. Then should the witness deny a fact you can impeach the witness.*

Re-examination:

After X, the party who called the witness may ask him further questions to clarify answers he provided or address new issues that arose in the X
Other parties may ask further questions.

ALWAYS REMEMBER TO KISS (KEEP IT SHORT AND SIMPLE)!!

In the wee hours of the morning, a lawyer called the governor of his state to inform him that a noted judge had just died and the lawyer wanted to take judge's place. The irritated governor wickedly assured him. "if it's okay with the funeral parlor, it's okay with me."

WORDS OF WISDOM

"Dignity does not consist in processing honours but in deserving them "– Aristotle

Appendix Grounds for objection

Info sought is irrelevant, unreliable, unnecessary or unfair
Questions repetitive or "bullying" in nature
Answer unreliable (i.e. based on hearsay or speculation
Answer outside witness's knowledge (ordinary witness asked an expert opinion
Opinions outside his area of expertise
Asking leading questions

Fools and obstinate men make lawyers rich.

CHAPTER 9

THE RULING

An understanding of the rules on rulings can go a long way to ensuring that the ruling is proper and has properly been arrived at.

The 7 C's of a ruling:

1. *Clear and Certain*
2. *Concise*
3. *Comprehensive*
4. *Competent*
5. *Consistent*
6. *Conclusive*
7. *Capable of Performance.*

General Rules:

- *Unless the parties otherwise agree, the decision of the majority of the members of a tribunal is the tribunal's ruling. If there is no majority, the decision of the chair is the ruling.*
- *Unless the parties agree otherwise, the dispute must be decided in accordance with the law and the hearing agreement, the contract under which the dispute arose and any applicable usages of trade.*
- *Unless the parties otherwise agree, ruling must be made in writing and must state the reasons it is based upon.*
- *Unless the parties otherwise agree, the tribunals can, in addition to damages, ruling:*
    i. *Specific performance (to require a party to perform a specific act), injunctions (an order restraining a person to perform a specific act) and other equitable remedies.*
    ii. *The cost of the hearing.*
    iii. *Pre ruling interest (in the same way as courts grant pre-judgement interest.*
    iv. *Tribunals have no power to ruling punitive or exemplary damages.*

I used to be a lawyer, but now I am a reformed character- Woodrow Wilson

WORDS OF WISDOM

**"My judgements prevent me from seeing the good that
lies beyond appearances"- Wayne Dyer**

A teacher an accountant and a lawyer were asked, "How much is four plus four?" the teacher answered "Eight!" The accountant said, "Seven or eight. I'll need to run that trough my spreadsheet for verification." The lawyer learned forward and whispered," How much do u want it to be?"

CHAPTER 10

CHALLENGES TO THE RULING.....

The courts will not interfere unless an injustice has been done. So what kind of injustice?

Over the years in most common law jurisdictions the courts are more and more reluctant to interfere in the arbitration process, except to prevent real injustice

There is a difference between setting aside a ruling and having a ruling remitted on various grounds. There are generally 6 specific grounds for remitting an ruling to an tribunal to reconsider the case:

i. *Where the ruling is ambiguous or uncertain or inconsistent with the hearing clause in the original contract providing for the ruling*

ii. *Where the tribunal has made a mistake and he/she has made a request for it to be remitted to him, for example to comply with the hearing agreement, mistakenly ruled on a payment to the wrong person or a mistake as to the principle on which the ruling is based*

iii. *There has been 'misconduct on the part of the tribunal'*

iv. *Material evidence which could not be obtained earlier with reasonable diligence has surfaced*

v. *Where an tribunal requests the court for a' question of Law" or "special case", and insufficient info has been provided by the said tribunal*

vi. *where there has been a" misunderstanding" causing injustice (although no "misconduct" by the tribunal).*

vii. *Where there has been non-compliance with legal requirements be they on procedural matters, or a significant matter in relation to the agreement between the parties.*

viii. *Where the tribunal has misdirected himself/herself and/or the proceedings. This may include proceedings ex parte (without sufficient cause, where the tribunal is excluding persons without sufficient cause, improperly receiving evidence or where there improper delegation of duties, by the said tribunal.*

When the attorney learned that his colleague of thirty years was dying, he hurried to the hospital. He found his friend struggling trough page after page of Holy Scripture. "Looking for solace, my friend?" he asked compassionately. "Nope." The dying man replied "loopholes."

A preacher found a signboard about to be changed and wrote at the bottom, I pray for all. A lawyer came later and wrote under that, I plead for all. A doctor saw the comments and wrote beneath, I prescribe for all. A common citizen finished the work with a final, I pray for all.

CHAPTER 11

RULES OF NATURAL JUSTICE OR PROCEDURAL FAIRNESS

Here are some basic rules on ensuring Procedural Fairness.

1. *The right to be heard*
2. *The right to an unbiased decision maker*

1. *THE RIGHT TO BE HEARD. (No single formula)*
    requirements for tribunals affected quite stringent

    I.e. requirements for oral hearing where all parties physically present

    X to be permitted.

    Amendment in 1990's written and electronic hearings allowed without consent as long as no prejudice to anyone.

    Interrogatories (a written question requiring an answer generally as if under oath) allowed in lieu of X.

    Notice of proceedings

    a. *With sufficient explanation to address issues*
    b. *Sufficient time to prepare*

    Limits on such rights:

    Of appeal held that tribunal cannot compel parties to disclose evidence in advance unless statute empowers it or procedural fairness rules require this On Human Rights Commission v. Dofasco Inc.

    -   *Right to be present throughout hearing*
    -   *And tribunal members may not discuss with one party alone.*
    -   *(In written hearings each party gets relevant information with the right to respond)*

- *In electronic hearings each party is to hear each other and the tribunal.*
All parties must be able to see video conference.

Limits on right to be present:

a. *If party served with notice and does not attend*
b. *Where party disrupting proceedings*
c. *If party "walks out"*
d. *Sensitivity of evidence and one party is too verbose*

NB: Advise parties early on such rights, intention of parties to be represented, time needed to find representation and efforts to be made
Parties not always entitled to 1st rep choice
Right to present evidence
To establish facts
Mechanism should be in place to allow the third party to provide info to a party
Limits to such rights
No right to present it ORALLY
Not if against rules of procedure or if irrelevant or unreliable
RIGHT TO X
Party must know evidence and to respond thereto.
Must be in good time and not irrelevant or unreliable.
(Includes written info)
X must not be inflammatory abusive or repetitive
SPPA and APA of BC provide reasonable rights to control procedures in this context.

2. *THE RIGHT TO AN UNBIASED DECISION MAKER.*

IMPARTIALITY

HE WHO HEARS MUST DECIDE IN AN UNFETTERED MANNER

EXCEPTION: prolonged illness or death, remaining members can render the decision. But some statutes require interest group to be present eg Union /Management.

Can make collegial decision making (of peers etc.). But the decision must be unfettered.

Decision must be based on submissions presented but entitled to "take notice" or "administrative notice" of well informed community member or professional group.

THE REQUIREMENTS TO GIVE REASONED DECISIONS

Generally required where an individual's rights, privileges, interests affected or to be able to appeal

All relevant Acts require it but in on where parties require reasons.

Test

- *Was there a reasonable apprehension of bias?*
  (Must be a reasonable one held by reasonable and right right-minded persons applying themselves to the question and obtaining thereon the required information).
- *Tribunal well informed, right-minded, practical and realistic. Relevant circumstances including the traditions of integrity and impartiality.*
- *There is a strong presumption of judicial integrity that can only be displaced by cogent contrary evidence*
- *Conflict of interest (e.g. financial or other interest) only one source of perceived bias*

INDICATORS OF BIAS:

- *- Meets with one party alone*
- *Close friendship/ relationship with 1 party*
- *Financial interest or association member*
- *Expresses opinion*
- *Intervenes in favour of one party or expresses a dislike*
- *Party to litigation against a party or witness*
- *Past bus or professional association*
- *Receives a gift*

Explanation:

- *Closeness in relationship with govt dept*
- *Multiple functions with overlap by employees*

Factors to gauge independence from govt:

i. *Appointment "at pleasure" or fixed term*
ii. *If fixed term, how long?*
iii. *Fixed salary (ok) or at will of govt*
iv. *Part time or full time (ok)*

v.   *Discretion of chair to appoint panel (not ok)*

vi.   *Employees appointed by govt (not ok)*

vii. *Requirement of tribunal to follow govt policy? (not ok)*

viii. *Minister evaluates chair? (not ok)*

ix.   *Govt. Funding? (not ok)*

Must be clear separation –investigating and admin action.

Argue case and admin decision.

CHAPTER 12

SOME CONSIDERATION OF MEETINGS IN GENERAL

What is a Meeting?

Each organizations constitution requires many matters to be carried out by resolution passed at a meeting it is frequently vital to know whether a meeting in the strict legal sense has been held. A meeting has been defined as a coming together for a common lawful object of two or more persons; and only in very exceptional circumstances as for example where all the shares of a class are held by one member or where the rules permit the appointment of a committee of one can a single person constitute a meeting. The general rule is that a single participant cannot form a meeting even if he/she has been appointed by all the other participants to represent them.

For a meeting of a constituted body to be valid, it must be:

> Properly convened;
> Properly constituted- with the right person in the chair and quorum present;
> Held in accordance in any applicable statutes and rules.

Quorum

A quorum is the minimum number of members who must be present before a meeting can validly transact business in the absence of any regulations at all two members are sufficient; (in companies the articles usually make provision and where they do not the companies act prescribes a minimum of three members for general meetings of a public company and two members for a private company.

The mere physical presence of a quorum without an intention to meet does not constitute of meeting.

Notice

Except where all the members of a body are present and all agree to waive notice a meeting can be held only if proper notice has been given the principal rules relating to notice are as follows:

Notice must be given to all those entitled to attend but rules frequently provide that accidental omission to give notice to a member shall not in validate the proceedings.

Notice must state the date, time and place of meeting all of which must be reasonably convenient.

Notice must be issued under proper authority

Notice must be served I n the manner provided e.g. by post

The proper length of notice must be given; and unless otherwise stated, clear days notice i.e. exclusive of the day of service and of the day of the meeting, must be given.

The notice must state fairly and frankly the nature of business to be transacted,

Chairman

The regulations usually provide who shall be chairman. Where they do not or the chairman is not present the meeting may elect one of their numbers. By so doing there devolves on him by agreement the conduct of the meeting subject to the applicable regulations.

A chairman should be impartial, well- informed with regard to procedure, courteous, good humored and fair but firm. He must in the first place see that the meeting has been properly convened and that it is duly constituted that his own appointment is in order and a quorum present; and he must preserve order and conduct the meeting regularly and se that the sense of the meeting is properly obtained on any question placed before it.

He must give all an equal opportunity to speak so far as time permits but when a matter has been adequately discussed he may close the discussion and put the motion to the vote.

He must see that all business is within the scope of notice and must not allow irrelevant discussion or improper language. It is his duty to decide who shall speak, to put motions and amendments to vote and to declare the result if the regulations provide he has an additional or casting vote to be used only on an equality of votes to secure a decision.

A chairman should deal with points of order as they are raised and having announced his decision e should maintain it.

The members have placed the control of themselves as individuals in his hands, and he is entitled to eject or have ejected any persons whose disorderly conduct prevents the transaction of business and who refuse to leave. (This power is to be exercised with due care, and the wishes of the meeting should be ascertained.) He is entitled to adjourn the meeting if necessary to preserve order, though here again the support of the majority present should be obtained.

Order on Debate

Companies (unlike legislative assemblies such as parliament) do not generally formulate standing orders to govern the conduct of their meetings, but they nevertheless observe certain rules based on custom. Thus the business should be taking order of the agenda unless the chairman varies the order in the constant of the meeting speakers stand when speaking except at the board and committee meetings and address the chair and must resume their seats if the chairman raises every member has generally a right to speak once but one only on each main motion and once on each amendment thereto but may move only one such amendment is before the meeting and all voting shall be by show or hands in the first place.

Motions and Amendments.

Strictly speaking a motion is proposition placed before a meeting which becomes only a resolution when adopted by the meeting; but the two terms are used almost synonymously.

Motions should always be couched in terms that are clear and definite and from ambiguity they should always be affirmative in form and commence with the word that so that when passed the record will read it was resolved that …. If the decision is to be immediately operative it should read be and is hereby done.

A motion must be within the scope of the notice convening the meeting and appropriate to the business of the meeting,

Generally a motion must be moved and seconded but although a chairman will usually require every motion to be seconded and will allow it to fall to the ground will not accept it for discussion if it does not find a seconder he is quite in order in putting an unseconded motion before the meeting unless the rules require otherwise. Motions are preferably committed to writing and handed to the chairman.

An amendment is a proposed alteration to a motion already under discussion by the meeting. It may take the form of adding words omitting words or substituting others or a combination of these it must conform to the general rules relating to motions except that it is not usually required to be seconded and it must not be a mere negation of the motion such as the insertion of word not a chairman has a discretion in accepting amendments, but once accepted, discussion must centre on such amendment until it is voted upon, when, if passed, it is incorporated in the main motion discussion the reverts to the motion or any further amendment which is dealt with similarly when the whole matter has been sufficiently discussed the motion as finally amended is put to the meeting as the substantive motion and if passed is ultimately incorporated in the minutes. The mover of the motion is usually allowed a right to reply to the debate before the motion is put to the vote but the right must be claimed an amendment does not give the mover any such right.

The Formal Motions

These are motions designed to secure the termination, different, or prevention of discussion of the particular business before the meeting. Properly used, they fulfill their function of expediting the transaction of business; for which the meeting was called and hence are sometimes termed dilatory motions. As a consequence the chairman has a wide discretion as to whether he accepts such a motion.

The principal formal motions are:

> ADJOURMENT OF THE MEETING. This may be moved by any member at the close of any speech. In the absence of any rule on the point it appears that a chairman must adjourn if the meeting resolves to do so; but the chairman may adjourn the meeting without asking a vote if he considers it necessary for the proper transaction of business, e.g, to await essential information. If he adjourns the meeting merely because things have taken a turn he does not like the meeting and no further notice need be sent out unless the regulations require, or unless the adjournment has been sine die (without fixing a day).

> ADJOURMENT OF THE DEBATE. This amounts to no more than the deferment of one item until later in the proceedings ex. until a related item has been settled.

> POSTPONEMENT. This amounts to the adjournment (of either a meeting or a motion) before discussion commences.

> PREVIOUS QUESTION. This is moved either in the form I move the previous question or I move that the question be now not put the intention is to shelve discussion on the whole subject i.e. the main motion and this is achieved by deciding either to put the matter to the vote at once, or to drop the whole matter for the meeting. This decision is the previous question the P.Q can be moved only when the main motion is before the meeting, and discussion on it is permitted. If the question is passed, the meting drops

the main motion and proceeds to the next business; if it is lost, the main motion is pit to the vote at once.

CLOSURE. This is usually in the form I move that the question be now put. It relates only to the particular motion or amendment before the meeting and is mostly used to curtail discussion or amendments. Hence, when moved and seconded, no discussion is allowed; the closure is put to the meeting and if, passed, the motion or amendment to "closure" is also put to the vote the mover if it is a main motion losing his right of reply. If the closure is lost discussion on the motion or amendment continues.

NEXT BUSINESS. A motion to "proceed with the next business" has the effect, if passed, of dropping the main motion before the meeting; and has no effect if lost.

CHAPTER 13

VOTING

The five usual methods of voting are:-

Voice or Acclamation. This can only be used where the meeting is practically unanimous.

Show of Hands. This is a method adopted at company meetings.

Poll. Literally a "counting of heads," but at company meetings each member has a number of votes laid down in the Articles, generally one vote for each share held.

Ballot. The members record their votes on voting papers, which they drip into a ballot box.

Division. The members pass out in separate rooms, being continued as they do so.

The chairman's declaration of the result of voting on a show of hands is conclusive unless a poll is demanded when the poll supersedes the original counting or unless there is some obvious error. At common law every member has a right to demand a poll; the demand must be made immediately upon the declaration of the result on the show of hands, and the chairman decides the time, manner and place of conducting the poll, subject to any regulations on the matter.

On a poll the votes of absent members may, if the regulations provide, be recorded by proxy.

CHAPTER 14

PRIVILEGE

Statements which injure a person's reputation if made orally constitute slander; and if the statement causes damage or alleges the commission of a criminal offense the person slandered may recover damages.

It is, however, essential that speakers at meetings should be free to talk frankly, without fear of being called to account in an action for slander; and accordingly, a person who in good faith makes a statement in pursuance of a duty to persons who have an interest in hearing the statement, or with a view to protecting his or his hearers interests is said to be protected by privilege. Such protection will be lost if the speaker is actuated by malice rather than duty or if he is a party to unnecessary publication e.g. he invites reporters to be present.

A "privileged occasion" is one where the above circumstances of duty and interest exist; meeting of directors and shareholders are consequently privileged occasions.

A written defamatory statement constitutes libel, and a civil action will lie without proof of damage. The protection of privilege applies as in the case of oral statements; consequently written reports made to a superior in the course of duty or placed before a board meeting are privileged if made in good faith, no matter how erroneous they may be.

To establish a prima facie case of libel it is necessary for the plaintiff to prove that the words complained of are defamatory and are therefore calculated to expose him to hatred, concept or ridicule or to cause him to be shunned or avoided;

> That they refer to the plaintiff; and

> That they are published by the defendant.

The following defenses are available in an action of defamation in speeches made at meetings or published reports thereof; unintentional defamation, fair comment (just and reasonable comment upon matters of the public interest, made without malice, privilege (absolute of qualified), and justification.

CHAPTER 15

PROCEDURE BEFORE, AT, AND AFTER MEETINGS

BEFORE studying the contents of this chapter, one is advised to read all matters referring to general meetings in any constitution to which he may have access.

The Annual General Meeting of an organization is usually held some three or four months after the conclusion of the financial year; in fixing the date, regard must be had not only for the obligation to hold a general meeting not later than fifteen months from the preceding general meeting. Accounts shall be laid before the members not more than eighteen months after incorporation and subsequently once at least in every calendar year. The meeting must be held within nine months of the date to which the accounts are made up.

When the accounts have been completed and audited, the secretary will proceed to draft the director's report which should be a plain statement of the results of the trading for the year, followed by a statement as to the allocation of profits between dividends, reserves and "carry forward". The report usually ends with a note as to the retiring directors and so to the auditors – whether the directors seek re-election, and whether (as usual) the auditors are to continue to serve until the next annual general meeting.

The secretary will see that the hall which it is proposed to use for the meeting is available for the contemplated date, and will then be in a position to have set up in type the various documents required to be send to members' entitled to attend the meeting; these will consist of the notice convening the meeting, the director's report, the Balance Sheet and Loss Account, and the auditors' report on Profit and Loss Account and Balance Sheet and on the group accounts (if any). Proofs of these will be obtained and submitted to a duly convened Board meeting, which the auditors' representative will be invited to attend.

At this meeting the directors or governing body will approve the various documents, and they will discuss with the auditors' representative any amendment they desire in the form of accounts as they are to be printed. These matters settled, they will pass resolutions:

Authorizing the signing of the governing bodies report by the chairman or the secretary on their behalf; authorizing the signing of the balance sheet by on behalf of the Governing body.

Convening the meeting and authorizing the meeting in the Press; if necessary.

As soon as this meeting is concluded, the secretary will instruct the printers to proceed with all the necessary printing. It will generally be necessary to obtain two final proofs of the report and accounts and, after having them signed by the directors as arranged, to send them to the auditors, who will retain one copy for their files and return the other with the auditors' report thereon duly signed. This copy should be carefully preserved and should be available at the annual appropriate meeting.

Envelopes will be prepared, ready to dispatch the report and accounts, etc., to all members of the organization.

The secretary will put in hand the chairman's detailed agenda for the meeting, and may be required to assist in the preparation of the chairman's speech.

A member entitled to attend and vote at a meeting may appoint another person to attend and vote in his place (who need not also be a member: needed, the member might send his advocated or his accountant, although in the case of meeting of a public company such a person has not the right to speak). The proxy forms should be checked and entered on a Proxy List as they are received; and the proxy forms and the list must be taken to the meeting.

Arrangements for the Meeting

On the day appointed for the meeting, the room must be prepared. Seats will be arranged for the chairman and the other directors at a tablet the head of the room and other seats will be provided for the general body of the shareholders. Where it is the practice to do so, copies of the agenda, reports and accounts of the directors and report of the auditors, will be placed on the seats for those attending. On the table, in front of the chairman, will be the fully detailed agenda, either on a loose leaf sheet or written in an Agenda Book, opened ready for the chairman's is. There will also be at hand the original signed copies of the report and accounts and auditors' report, correspondence to be read at the meeting, and the draft of the chairman's speech. The secretary will have at hand the Minute book, copy of the agenda (detailed), a copy of the report and auditors' report, the signed notice convening the meeting, and any other documents he may consider necessary. At every meeting he should have with a copy of th constitution of the company.

There should also be Available is a good supply of writing materials. If the meeting is one important to the general public, reporters may be present, who should be afforded proper facilities.

The room should be open for the admission of shareholders at least half hour before the time appointed for commencing the meeting. As the members enter the room, their attendance will automatically be recorded by their presenting admission cards. Where a card system is not adopted, arrangements should be made to take the signatures of those attending as they enter the room.

The chairman, and other directors, together with the secretary, and, where usual, other officers, e.g. the general manager, should be in their places before the advertised time of the meeting, so as to ensure its starting promptly. This applies also to any members of the staff who may be assisting.

If at the appointed hour the chairman finds that a quorum be not present, the meeting must stand adjourned, or as the constitution directs.

The constitution should ideally provide for a quorum of "three members present in person," and provides, further, that if a quorum is not present within half an hour of the time fixed for the following week, and at the same place; and if at such adjourned meeting there is no quorum within half an hour of members present will constitute the quorum. If, however, it be a meeting specially convened upon the requisition of members, it must be dissolved.

Assuming that a quorum is present, the chairman will customarily call upon the secretary to read the notice convening the meeting. The next item is the reading of the auditors' report upon the accounts; this duty is occasionally undertaken by the representative of the auditors but is more usually carried out by the secretary. The report and accounts of the governing body comes next, and it is usual for the chairman to ask the members, in view of the fact that these documents have been in their hands for the relevant period, to take them as read; a formal request to which there is seldom any dissent. He will proceed to move the adoption of the report and accounts by reading out the motion from the detailed agenda sheet. He then proceeds to deliver his "chairman's speech," in which he may review the year's activity, draw attention to any special points in the accounts, and possibly express an opinion of the prospects of the company for the immediate future. On the conclusion of his speech he calls upon the person named in the agenda to second the resolution. This gentleman (or possibly lady) will usually read the terms of the resolution from a slip which has been previously handed to him by the secretary, and may speak at length or otherwise on the matter. Following him, the shareholders, who are entitled to discuss the report and accounts, are asked by the chairman if they have any questions to ask or remarks to make in regard to have the report and accounts. This is the opportunity of dissatisfied and other member and where a satisfactory report has not been presented, numerous questions may be asked as to the affairs of the company, and an application may be made for an investigation into the company's affairs.

Putting the Resolution to the Meeting

A resolution is put to the meeting by the chairman saying, "Those in favor?" whereupon every member who vote for the resolution holds up a hand. If there is any case for believing a count to be necessary, the hands so held up will be counted by the chairman. The counting concluded, he will say, "Those against?" and the procedure will be repeated. Where it is a foregone conclusion that the resolution will be carried by a large majority, or the hands held up "in favor" show conclusively that the meeting is in favor of the resolution, the counting will be omitted unless, of course, it is necessary to ascertain that the resolution has been passed by a certain majority. In such a case, however, there is usually a poll, as proxies have to be allowed for. The chairman may declare a resolution as carried, or by a certain majority, or where all have voted for the motion, carried unanimously; again, where no one has voted against the motion, carried men. Con. (nominee contradicente).

A member dissatisfied with the declaration may call for a count, or a recount, as the case may be; or he may resort at once to his right to demand a poll.

CHAPTER 16

PROXIES

Constitutions usually require that an instrument appointing a proxy to vote at a meeting confers the authority to demand a poll. The word proxy is used to indicate both the person voting by proxy and the instrument authorizing him to vote; but the present writer prefers to use the terms as meaning only the person acting for another. A proxy may be any person, whether a member or not. A proxy appointed to attend and vote has the same right as the member to speak at the meeting

When a poll is taken, as the case may be, scrutineers are often appointed by the meeting, whose business it is to report to the chairman the result of voting. Their work will be greatly facilitated by the secretary having at hand a list of proxies and the votes represented by them, and the Register of Members of those present at the meeting. The latter should be signed by the scrutineers before being handed to the chairman.

Under some constitution, no a person in arrears of dues or of unsound mind, or in respect of whom an order has been made by any court having jurisdiction in lunacy, may vote, whether on a show of hands, or on poll, by his trustee, and such trustee may, on a poll; vote by proxy.

CHAPTER 17
RECORDS OF THE MEETING

During the progress of the meeting the secretary will have been taking brief notes of the proceedings. At a meeting of members he will usually have little to do in this respect. Against each item on the agenda he will put a tick to indicate that the matter referred to was passed. Where information has been asked for and promised by the chairman, he will make a note of this, also of any suggestions made by shareholders to the Board. Where the resolutions were passed in the form drafted by the secretary he will not need to copy them in his notes, nor will it be necessary for him to put the names of the proposers and secondary of resolutions therein, if they are those originally arranged for. If, of course, any instructions have been given at the meeting, it is the duty of the secretary to see that they are noted and carried out.

The secretary's first duty after meeting of members is to write up the record of the proceedings-the minutes- and as has been pointed out in a preceding chapter, everything material must be included in the minutes, before entry, should be submitted to the chairman for his approval, and after entry, the minutes should be laid before the next Board meeting and is signed by the chairman thereof. Where it is the custom, copies of the "Report of the Proceedings" will be printed and sent to the members. In the case of directors absent from the meeting and who have been re-elected, a notification should be sent to them. After such a meeting, too, there is the important work of posting the Dividend Warrants and of making up and forwarding the Annual Return

CHAPTER 18

BOARD OF GOVERNORS MEETINGS

Although there is less formality at such meetings than at general meetings, it is nevertheless just as important that the requirements of the law and the constitution are strictly observed.

The constitution usually permit the governing body to "regulate their meetings as they think fit." Unless, however, they have arranged to meet at fixed intervals and to dispense with notice, reasonable notice (say, two or three days at least) must be given of every meeting. If, however, all the members are, in fact, present and agree, they can waive notice. This does not mean that because all they happen to be present, they can force one of their numbers, against his will, to take part in a meeting on the spot; but on the other hand, where they are all present and agree, they can hold a meeting in the most informal circumstances – e.g. on a railway platform, conversing through carriage window of a train about to depart. A constitution often states that a written resolution, signed by all the directors for the time being entitled to receive notice of such a meeting, shall be valid and effectual without an actual meeting being held.

The constitution should state what the quorum for a Board meeting is, and it must be remembered that any business conducted without quorum, unless subsequently ratified, may be invalid. Moreover, there is a common law rule which prevents members who are interested in a contract with the organization both from voting on the matter and from being counted in the quorum." The constitution may however, amend this rule; but where the member abstains from voting on a contract because he is interested in it, it is as well to record the fact in the minutes, thus:

"Mr. A. B., being interested in the firm of C. And Co., abstained from voting."

Even if the Articles allow him to vote, an interested director must disclose at a Meeting the nature of his interest in any contract with the company. A general notice that he is a member of a particular firm or company, and is to be regarded as interested in any contract therewith, is usually sufficient.

The careful secretary will endeavor to keep in mind any interests so declared; for in the event of the absence of a dis-interested quorum, or the improper inclusion of such a director's vote, the contract may be avoided by the other party.

There will also be the preparation of the agenda and the forwarding of a copy of it, where the practice exists, to each director. With the notice, the secretary should send a note of reminder to any director whose duty it is to present any information to the meeting. In the preparation of the room a supply of writing materials should be placed before each director. The secretary will have at hand a copy of the Memorandum and the constitution, the Minute Book, Attendance Book, copies of the agenda and all documents to be dealt with at the meeting. All papers can best be handled by the secretary if they are properly marked for identification.

On the chairman taking his seat at the meeting begins after which the secretary is called upon to read the minutes of the last meeting. This done, the chairman says, "You have heard the minutes of the last meeting read. Will someone move that they be approved?"

The proposer and seconder of the resolution affirming the correctness of the minutes will, of course, be persons who attended the meeting to which the minutes refer. Where an error has been made it must be corrected.

After the minutes have been read, they are signed by the chairman, who, at the same time, should affix the date of the signing.

The next item on the agenda is usually "Matters arising out of the Minutes." This enables the chairman or the secretary, to explain that certain instructions have been carried out, or to explain how far matters in a certain direction have progressed. The arrangement of the business should, as far as possible, be in accordance with the agenda, but the chairman may and often does alter this as he consider fit, particularly where by accident the secretary has not placed adjacent to each other matters having similar bearing. Another reason may be that the chairman wishes to ensure the consideration of some special matter. But it should be noted that, strictly speaking, the order of business should not be altered without the consent of the meeting.

CHAPTER 19

THE SECRETARY'S NOTES

The notes that the secretary will take of the proceedings of the meeting will consist largely of decisions for incorporation in the minutes, and instructions which he will be responsible for carrying out. Naturally, the secretary will adopt the briefest of methods, when making his notes.

The initial after each note refers to the proposer and seconder.

At the conclusion of the meeting, the secretary will find that the list of instructions is frequently a large one, and if this be the case, he will be advised to have his "reminders" reproduced and written in triplicate form. One copy will be sent to the person concerned, at once, and another will be put in the secretary's "tickler" while the third copy will be retained for general reference. The "tickler" copy may be sent to the director as a further reminder of the duty he has to accomplish- with the notice convening the next meeting of directors. As soon as possible the minutes will be drafted for the chairman's approval and entered in the Minute Book.

In most constitution there will be regulations for the conduct of directors' meetings but apart from the meetings, members of committees may have a large amount of work to do before they can report to the general body of directors, who confirm or otherwise the recommendations they make in regard to the matter which they were specifically appointed to consider. It should be clearly understood however, that committees of the Board can be appointed only when the constitution authorize such appointment. The constitution usually provides for delegation of powers to committees.

CHAPTER 20
NOTICES OF MEETINGS

A general meeting may be called notice in writing; and any other general meeting (except one for passing a resolution) A meeting to pass a special resolution needs notice as provided for in the constitution refer to notices for company meetings and provide for the above-mentioned notices exclusive of the day on which notice is served or deemed to be served, but inclusive of the day for which the notice is given and specifying the place, day and hour of meeting. Where special business is to take place, particulars must be stated in the notice, which must be sent to every member or person entitled, but non-receipt of the notice by any member shall not invalidate the proceedings in any general meeting.

The constitution will usually provide that notices may be served personally or be sent by post to the registered address of the shareholder, and will be deemed to be properly served if the letter containing the notice is correctly addressed, prepaid and posted, unless proof of the contrary is established. Where the registered address of the shareholder is not in the country, he should supply an address within the country to which notices can be sent if this is possible. Where shares are held jointly, the practice is to give notice to the one whose names appears first on the register. Secretaries will note that provision is made for the forwarding of the notices of meetings to persons entitles to shares in the consequence of death or bankruptcy of a member.

Notices of general meetings are invalid unless issued under the instructions of a properly constituted Board meeting, and the secretary should therefore see that the Board meeting at which it is decided to call a general meeting is itself validly convened, and that a quorum of directors is present.

The regulations with regard to the serving of notices for BOG meetings are usually conspicuous by their absence, or comprehend in the words, "the BOG may meet together for the dispatch of business, adjourn or otherwise regulate their meetings as they think fit." Nevertheless, the general rule is to forward written or unwritten notices a few days prior to the meeting taking place. In some companies no notice is served, the directors attending on a fixed day of a week or month. However, in practice, various papers for perusal by the directors are circulated before most Board meetings, which imply an imminent Board meeting even if formal notice is not enclosed. The business method is to have regulations so framed that written notice must be given at least two or three days before the meeting, with the reservation that a director or secretary may summon a meeting at any time, in a matter of urgency, at shorter notice.

CHAPTER 21

AGENDA

Agenda means "things to be done". Its commercial interpretation is "business to be transacted at a meeting." It is simply a statement of matters that have to be discussed at a meeting. At every meeting the chairman and the secretary at least should have a copy of it; at BOG meetings each member should have a copy; at meeting of members, the usual provision is to include the agenda in the notice convening the meeting. It is of general advantage for particulars to be attached likewise to the notices convening the meetings BOGs, so as to enable the latter to give some consideration to the matters referred to, before the meetings.

The more general practice in connection with director's meetings is to provide loose agenda sheets. Where an agenda book is used, the agenda items entered therein are placed before the chairman, and are regarded as the agenda. Those placed before the other directors or shareholders are copies only. As far as possible, matters of the similar character should be placed next to each other in any agenda, but in order in which the various matters will be dealt with at the meeting may be varied by the chairman, with the consent of those present.

There are two recognized method of preparing the agenda. Paper; one method is to enter the bare outline or summary of a various items to be considered on the left-hand side, leaving a wide margin on the right-hand side in which the chairman and secretary will record notes of the decision arrived by at the meeting, these notes forming the basis of preparation of the minutes. In the second method fuller details are given, including draft of the resolution to be submitted, and the agenda is so worded that, by the alteration of few words, the agenda paper will form the draft minutes, thus facilitating the subsequent writing up of the minutes book. This method is useful for routine work at Board meetings as the director can see at a glance exactly what business is to be transacted.

The agenda of the meeting of members is where the organization issues a printed report, attached to it, but for the purpose of the chairman and secretary, a more detailed form should be made.

Once the minutes have been written up and signed by the chairman as the correct, the agenda paper may be destroyed. This, in fact, is the recommended procedure, because retention to the agenda, with its rough notes, means that two separate records of the same meeting will exist, one being necessarily of a rather hurried and imprecise nature. Carefully prepared and accurate minutes are all that is required

CHAPTER 22
RESOLUTIONS

A resolution may be defined as a formal decision by vote of a legislative or other body; a motion is a proposal placed before a meeting with a view to its adoption as a resolution. Strictly speaking, therefore, motions and resolutions are not the same things.

In studying this section of the subject of the meetings the reader must be very careful to note the kinds of resolutions, the reasons for them and the framing of them.

Ordinary Resolution

An ordinary resolution is one which is passed by a simple majority of those present who are entitled to vote and who vote at a meeting. Such a resolution is used for the disposal of any business not requiring, under the constitution, to be passed by any other kind of resolution. It is thus used for all ordinary business at extraordinary general meetings.

Extraordinary Resolution

Extraordinary resolution is defined by the company's act. A resolution shall be an extraordinary resolution when it has been passed by a majority of not less than ¾ of such members as, being entitled so to do, vote in person or, where proxies are allowed, by proxy, at a general meeting at which notice specifying the intention to propose the resolution as an extraordinary resolution has been duly given.

Framing of resolution

The majority of the resolution will be framed by the secretary, no matter to what meetings they refer; but they should be noted: unless the matter is perfectly cleared that is advisable for most special and extraordinary resolutions to be drafted by the company's advocate. When it is remembered for what purposes such as resolutions are purposed, it will be realized how possible it is to frame a resolution detrimental to the interest of the company. In many cases that matters to which such resolutions refer are such as will generally have to be dealt by an advocate, and in that event he will undoubtedly frame any necessarily resolutions.

Occasionally also, important decisions of the Board in respect in which is essential that they are technically correct from the legal aspect, should be incorporated by the advocates in the resolutions to be passed by the Board; these These observations apart, it will be found that capable secretary will have no difficulty in the framing of resolutions in general. In so doing, he must bear following facts in mind:-

The object of the resolution.

The necessity of framing it in language at once clear and unmistakable; any ambiguity might defeat the object of the resolution.

The resolution must be in accordance with the Constitution This means, inter alia, that the effect of it must not be ultra virus i.e. something beyond the power of the company to adopt.

The particular wishes of the chairman BOG

In regard to this last, it is a practice in some companies to submit to the chairman all resolutions to be purposed before the meeting, where possible.

Bearing the above matters in mind, the secretary will proceed in the framing of the resolution thus:-

Marshal the facts, in having done so-

Summarize them, and-

Incorporate them in a plainly worded and decisive statement.

Rescission

A resolution is rescinded at a meeting at which it has been passed. If a cancellation is decided upon, the resolution should be rescinded at a later meeting.

Majority

The word "majority" has two meanings:

A number which is more than half of the whole number

The number by which the votes of one side exceed those of the others.

CHAPTER 23

MINUTES

A MINUTE as defined in the dictionary is "A note to assist the memory." In business matters, minutes are records of proceedings at meetings. Limited companies are required to "Cause minutes of all proceedings, all proceedings at meetings of its directors, and, where there are managers to be entered in the books kept for that purpose;" and further, "Any such minute purporting to be signed by the chairman of the meeting at which the proceedings were had, or, by the chairman of the next succeeding meeting, shall be evidence of the proceedings." Where such minutes are not kept, the company and every officer in default shall be liable to the default fine. Apart from the necessity of observing the above requirements it will be evident to all that records of proceeding must be kept in order to "assist the memory" of the directors and shareholders of the company and in regards to the matter they regularly discussing.

Kinds of Minutes

An examination of the minutes that is of the records proceedings will reveal the fact that such minutes contain-

Statement of fact or circumstance, sometimes called Minutes of Narration and

Resolutions or statements of decision.

A Minute of Narration may either stand alone or be attached to a resolution as the circumstances determine.

The Minute Book

Separate books should be used for minutes and the committee meetings, each with sheets consecutively numbered, and provided with an extension index. The latter will refer to all the minutes recorded, but in place of this the card index system may be and often is used. Minutes relating to more than one meeting should not be entered on the same page. Many forms contain only two divisions, one for the number of minutes and the other, the larger portion, for all other particulars. Sometimes, the names of proposer and seconder are given. In a column marked "subject", a very brief statement of what the minutes refers to will be given, while in the "Reference Index" column will be entered a reference to the pages of the book which, before and after the minute referred to contain any reference to the same subject matter. This index will be used only in matters of importance occurring frequently. Instead of referring to pages, the number might refer to minutes, but it would be desirable in that case to have the matter numbered consecutively throughout the book.

Before minutes are recorded in the Minute Book, it is a good plan, where possible, to show a rough draft to the chairman, for his approval. This will usually do away with the necessity of having to alter the minutes where the secretary has misunderstood some direction of the minutes. Where a mistake has been made in entering the minutes, before they are signed it will be better for secretary to rule neatly through the error, and re-enter the particulars correctly. He should get his chairman to initial the deletions when the minutes are being signed. If the minutes are being typed on unnumbered loose-leaf sheets, or in digital form it is, of course, possible to re-type them. No erasures of any kind must be made. After the minutes are signed, the proper course, where a mistake has been made, is to pass a resolution rescinding the minute referred to, making the corrected on accordingly.

Whilst a narration should precede a resolution wherever necessary to explain the circumstances in which it came to be passed, the secretary should avoid so far as possible the minting of reason; for the reason which actuated one director to vote for a resolution maybe the very reason why another director voted against it. Moreover, it is usual to record only the fact that the resolution was passed, without indicating the numbers voting for or against; but it is generally accepted that a director who disagrees with any particular decision has the right, if he wishes, to have the fact of his voting against, or abstention from voting, recorded in the minutes.

Proposals which were not accepted are usually omitted from minutes, unless the matter happens to be of exceptional importance.

Reading the Minutes

The customary practice is for the minutes of one board meeting to be read at the next board meeting and, after being read, the chairman asks his co-directors if the minutes as read are correct record. Upon their assent being obtained, the chairman adds his signature and the date. The minutes of annual meetings are usually approved at the next succeeding board meeting. Where this course is adopted no reference is made at the annual general meeting to the previous year's minutes.

CHAPTER 24

REPORTS

THE secretary will have to frame the following among other reports-

The Statutory Report.

The report of the directors to the shareholders on results of trading-commonly known as the Annual Report.

Report or summary of the proceedings of important meetings of the company, where such are provided for the issue to the shareholders or to the press, e.g. report of the annual general meeting.

Reports of committees of directors on special matters.

Reports of BOG Committees

Committees of BOG's may be classed thus-

Standing or permanent committees.

Committees which exist only for the purpose of undertaking special business.

Not all BOG's have standing committees, and some organizations have no committee at all. The articles must authorize the formation of a committee before it can be appointed.

The most familiar instance of a standing committee of an organization is a Finance Committee.

Reports of Committees of BOG's on Special Matters

There are of very varied character, but the following brief list will give an idea of the matters often reported on-

The desirability of opening business in another marketing area.

The advisability of erecting new premises.

The purchase of another business undertaking.

To consider the raising of additional capital.

To inquire into the management of certain departments.

To co-operate with other business undertakings in the promotions of legislation in a certain direction.

The establishment of a Pensions Funds for employees.

In arranging a set of "heads" as guidance when formulating the report, consideration must be given to the particular nature of the matter to be reported on. Thus, in some cases the following "heads" would be suitable-

> The terms of the resolution, that is, a copy of the resolution of the directors, with the date when passed.

> A statement of the inquires made or particulars of advice sought for and from whom.

> Tests and results of any tests, where made (as in witnessing the tests of strengths of materials, yarns, cloths, etc.,' or

Again, materials used in the construction of erection of buildings, etc.)

> The general finding of the committee, and where the members are divided in their opinion, the nature and causes of the division of opinion.

Printed in the United States
by Baker & Taylor Publisher Services